Science Technology Engineering Math
STEM STARTERS FOR KIDS
STEAM

ART
ACTIVITY
Book

Packed with activities and art facts

Written by Jenny Jacoby

Designed and illustrated by Vicky Barker

FOR YOUNG READERS

Racehorse for Young Readers

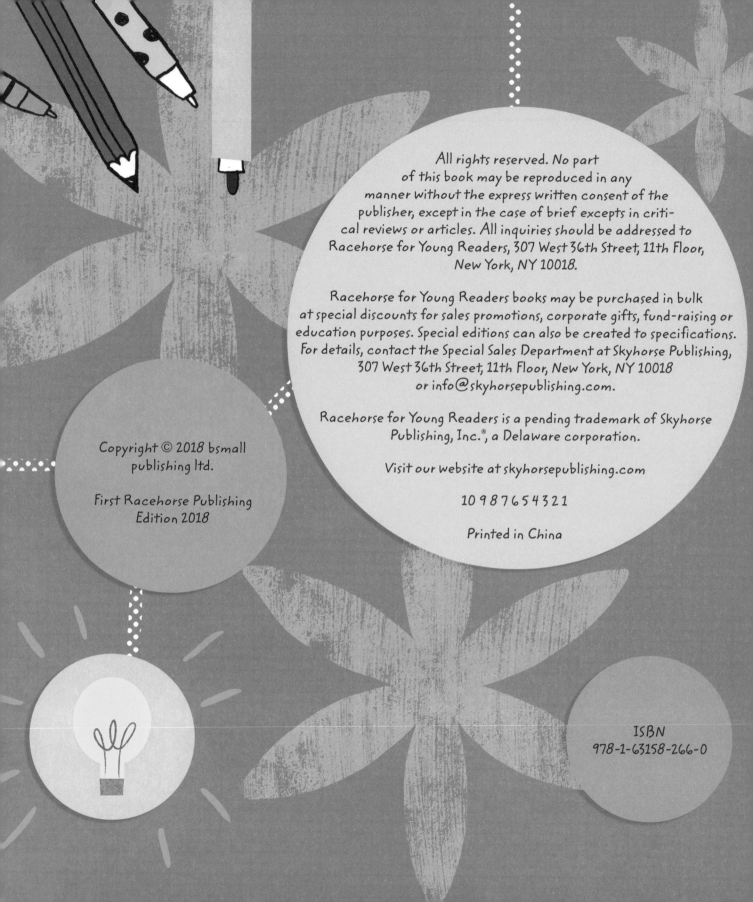

Racehorse for Young Readers books may be purchased in bulk
at special discounts for sales promotions, corporate gifts, fund-raising or
education purposes. Special editions can also be created to specifications.
For details, contact the Special Sales Department at Skyhorse Publishing,
307 West 36th Street, 11th Floor, New York, NY 10018
or info@skyhorsepublishing.com.

Racehorse for Young Readers is a pending trademark of Skyhorse
Publishing, Inc.®, a Delaware corporation.

Visit our website at skyhorsepublishing.com

10 9 8 7 6 5 4 3 2 1

Printed in China

Copyright © 2018 bsmall
publishing ltd.

First Racehorse Publishing
Edition 2018

ISBN
978-1-63158-266-0

WHAT IS ART?

Art is a creative expression of some thought, feeling or experience. Artists use a huge range of techniques to get their message across, from drawing and painting, to sculpture, writing and dance. Artists are inspired by all sorts of things in the world, and use all sorts of tools to create their work. Sometimes that involves technology (anything from a pencil to a camera or a 3D printer) and if the tool they need doesn't exist yet, sometimes artists even invent their own technology!

WHAT IS STEAM?

STEM stands for 'science, technology, engineering and mathematics.' These four areas are closely linked, and adding art puts in an 'A' to make STEAM. Art techniques and ways of thinking can inspire technology, just as technology, science and math can inspire art. Together, STEAM can help solve problems and make our lives better in ways nobody has even thought of yet

Science   Technology   Engineering   Art   Math

COMPLEMENTARY COLORS

Understanding color is so important for artists. Look at these pairs of colors. Three of them look lively next to each other and three of them look dull together. The lively pairs are called **complementary colors** and they make each other zing because they are so different. Colors that are more similar don't bring out the best in each other. The physics of color can explain how this works.

Dull - - - →

Complementary - - - ↑

4

This is a color wheel but it is only half full: only the three primary colors have been filled in. Use the rules to complete the color wheel with your coloring pens.

The Rules

Fill in the empty space with the color made by mixing the two primary colors either side of that space.

blue + yellow = ?

yellow + red = ?

blue + red = ?

The colors you are adding in are called the **'secondary colors'** because they are made from the primary colors. Do you notice anything about the complementary color pairs? Check your answer at the back of the book.

OPTICAL ILLUSIONS

Our eyes often deceive us. Artists have come up with many ways to show us how our eyes and brain try to trick us – while scientists have shown why those tricks work.

Our eyes send messages to our brains about what we are seeing. Our brains have learned to apply what we already know about the world to the messages our eyes send, to make sense of what we see. Sometimes that means our brains have to invent things that we are not actually seeing. For example, this apple is not just the half part that we can see, but is a whole apple behind another object.

Babies have to learn this — it is not something we are born knowing how to do!

Can you believe your eyes with these optical illusions?

Which of these lines is longer?

How many triangles are in this picture?

Are these lines parallel?

Is the dot on the front of the box or the back?

Are the horizontal lines straight or sloping?

7

TESSELLATION

When shapes **fit together** perfectly it is called tessellation.
The simplest tessellating shape is a box, but that isn't very interesting.

Circles don't tessellate as there are these gaps left in between.

Color in these tessellating shapes.

1. Color the first one in red and the one next to it in green. Alternate them in red and green to see the tessellating pattern.

2. Color the first one in blue and the one next to it in yellow. Alternate them in blue and yellow.

3. Color the first one in purple, and the one next to it in orange. Alternate them in purple and orange.

Now try making your own tessellating shapes! Use the dots to create a shape, then draw its partners around it to show it tessellating. You can it as unusual a shape as you like, but the simpler the shape the easier it is to make it work.

INFOGRAPHICS

Some ideas can be complicated to explain to others, perhaps because they contain lots of different ideas to remember at once, or involve lots of numbers. A brilliant way to explain something complex or long is by using infographics. Infographics is just a fancy way of saying that you're using pictures and diagrams to explain some information. The main idea is that an infographic looks nice and provides information. And sometimes that is just a better way to communicate an idea than a list of facts and figures.

In our class the children have a lot of different hobbies.

HOBBY	NUMBER OF CHILDREN	REASON FOR LIKING
Ballet	3	"I like ballet because I feel graceful and get to leap around"
Football	18	"I love to run around with my friends and it's best when I score a goal"
Arts & crafts	7	"It is exciting to start with miscellany and end up with something great"
Swimming	10	"Swimming makes me feel really happy"
Cycling	20	"Cycling feels like magic when I go fast downhill"

Here is the information as an infographic.

"I like ballet because I feel graceful and get to leap around"

"I love to run around with my friends and it's best when I score a goal"

"Swimming makes me feel really happy"

"It is exciting to start with miscellany and end up with something great"

"Cycling feels like magic when I go fast downhill"

Can you complete this infographic about the ways children travel to school? Make it look as colorful or simple as you like but use the spaces to get across the information in your own way. Remember: the bigger the shape, the more children it represents doing that activity.

TRANSPORT	NUMBER OF CHILDREN	REASON
Walk	19	"I like to walk to school with my friends."
Cycle	5	"I like cycling because I can go quicker."
Scooter	4	"I like to whizz past the people walking to school."
Car	2	"My mom drives me to school then drives to work"

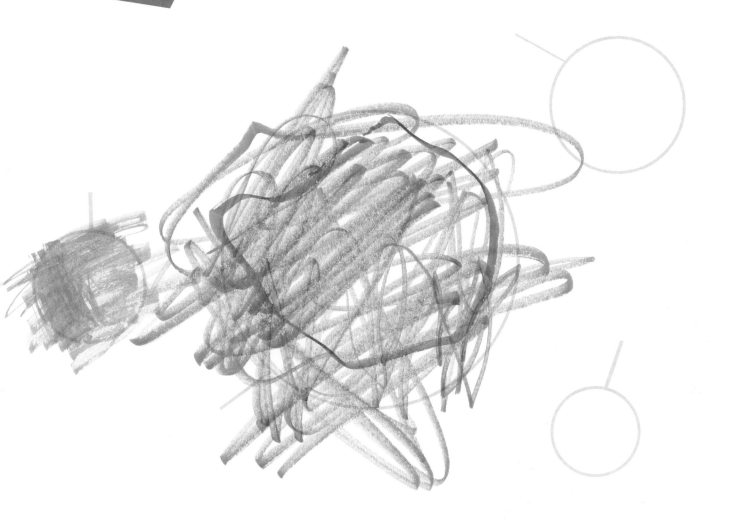

SKETCHING

An art skill that can really help to communicate your ideas is sketching. This can be useful for anybody working in a team who has an idea the whole group should understand, and sometimes drawing the idea can be the quickest way to express it.

Practice sketching by really looking at your subject.

Remember: don't worry about making your sketch perfect — any kind of sketch is useful, and the word 'sketch' means it isn't perfect.

Three tips:

Be free —
draw what you see without thinking too much about it.

Draw big —
use as much of the paper as you can.

Sketch lightly first —
that way you can rub out any lines you don't like.

What shapes make up the object?

2. Start by drawing the biggest simple shapes.

3. Then add in detail.

Try sketching these objects, following the same steps.

CONTINUOUS LINE DRAWING

Anyone can draw a face – but can you draw one without taking your pencil off the paper? It can be fun to add a rule to your drawing, to make it a bit harder and test your skills. Scientists and engineers might have all sorts of logical problems to solve with rules that change with each different project.

An artist called Alexander Calder was famous for continuous line drawings – that means drawing a picture without taking the pencil off the paper – and he had some advice:

- Draw slowly, and don't take the pencil from the paper until the whole picture is finished

- Your line can loop about and cross over itself to shape the whole picture

- These drawings take practice! Try drawing the same picture a few different ways.

Practice your adaptability to new rules by drawing these figures as continuous lines to make them more of a challenge!

THE SHAPE GAME

Scientists and engineers always need to be creative – they need to think up new questions to answer, and clever ways to solve problems. Being creative is something you can get better and better at the more you practice – and the shape game is a very fun way to practice letting your imagination fly!

Color me in!

Use pencils and colors to change these random shapes into something wild from your imagination. You can add bits on and adapt it how you like, but use the shape given to spark an idea.
Here's one example.

17

MIND MAPS

A mind map is a drawing of an idea. It is a way to draw all your thoughts about an idea in one place – and that can help you to see links you hadn't thought about. This could be useful for a team of scientists or engineers trying to solve a problem or come up with new ideas. Why just have a list when you could have a beautiful mind map that you might even want to hang on your wall and look at? Here's how.

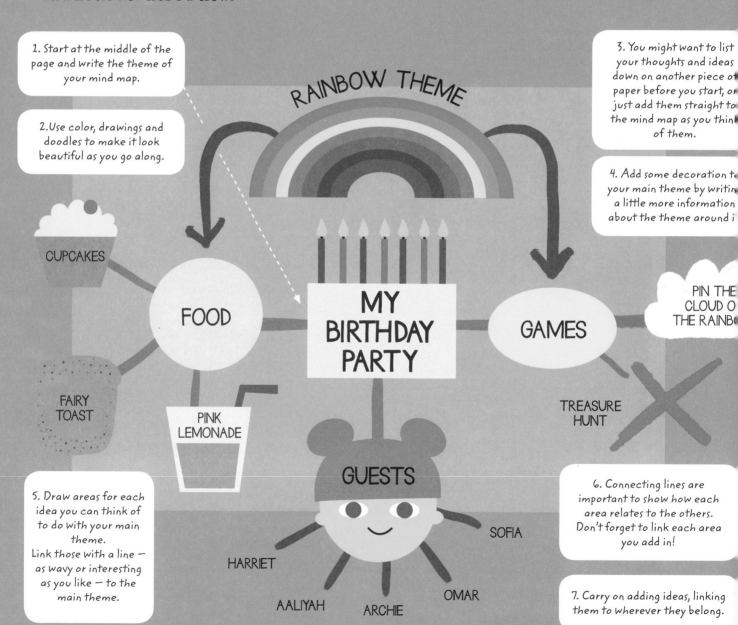

1. Start at the middle of the page and write the theme of your mind map.

2. Use color, drawings and doodles to make it look beautiful as you go along.

3. You might want to list your thoughts and ideas down on another piece of paper before you start, or just add them straight to the mind map as you think of them.

4. Add some decoration to your main theme by writing a little more information about the theme around i[t]

5. Draw areas for each idea you can think of to do with your main theme.
Link those with a line – as wavy or interesting as you like – to the main theme.

6. Connecting lines are important to show how each area relates to the others. Don't forget to link each area you add in!

7. Carry on adding ideas, linking them to wherever they belong.

RAINBOW THEME

CUPCAKES

FOOD

MY BIRTHDAY PARTY

GAMES

PIN THE CLOUD O[N] THE RAINB[OW]

FAIRY TOAST

PINK LEMONADE

TREASURE HUNT

GUESTS

HARRIET

AALIYAH

ARCHIE

OMAR

SOFIA

This mind map is looking rather boring. Use colors and doodles to decorate it and fill it in for your holiday plans.

HAVE FUN OUTDOORS

MY HOLIDAY

THINGS TO SPOT

FOOD

GAMES

DRAWING FOR CONCENTRATION

Sometimes when you really need to get your thinking cap on to concentrate on solving a problem, it is helpful to keep your hands busy. It allows the rest of your brain to focus on deeper thinking.

These colorful mandala-inspired patterns are a great way to keep your hands busy and your mind creative. Starting with a series of concentric circles (that means, circles getting bigger but all with the same center) fill in each row with different colorful patterns.

'Mandala' is the Sanskrit word for 'circle' and is a drawing that represents the universe.

Try creating your own designs here. One has been started for you. Use the circles as guidelines and draw in whatever shapes you choose: circles, triangles, loops, dots, raindrops ... The important part is to repeat your shapes in each section, using the lines as guides.

DRAWING DATA

When scientists do research they come up with 'data' – the numbers and results of their research. Often this data will be in a table or a list. While that information can be very useful it is not always going to look very interesting. A table of data is the purest way of presenting information, but information could be presented in as many ways as you can imagine.

Here are a few different ways to show the information about what this family ate for dinner last night. These are simple versions of the infographics on page 10.

1: A description

"Last night Daddy cooked spaghetti bolognese for us all to eat, but Mommy said she only wanted some soup, and my two brothers wanted their favorite food instead, so in the end only Dad and I ate pasta, and my brothers had fish sticks and scrambled eggs."

2: A table

PERSON	FOOD
Mom	Soup and bread
Dad	Spaghetti bolognese
Phoebe	Spaghetti bolognese
Harry	Fish sticks, french fries, pea
Leo	Scrambled egg on toast

3: A picture

Mom Dad Phoebe Harry Leo

Can you use the information in the table to draw in the fruit and vegetables on sale at the grocery store?

Oranges	5
Strawberries	10
Carrots	9
Potatoes	15
Apples	4
Leeks	6

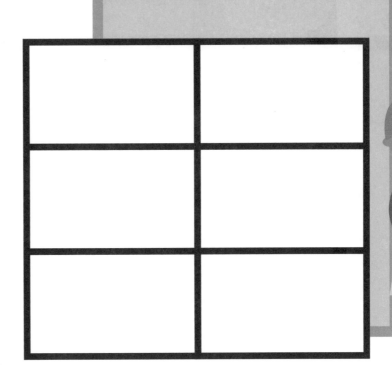

Soup and bread : 20%

Scrambled eggs on toast : 20%

Color in the pie chart — choose a different color for each section of the 'pie.' Perhaps you could choose a color similar to the food it represents.

Fish, fries, peas : 20%

Spaghetti Bolognese : 40%

PERFORMANCE

Another form of art is performance, using your body or voice to express an idea. An important part of science is observation. Once you have observed something – for example, how a cat moves when it is chasing a mouse – you can try to perform what you have seen. Acting out what you have observed can help you to understand it better and remember it for longer.

These people are performing different things. Can you match the performers to the ideas they are expressing?

25

SPIRALS

There are so many
examples of spirals in
nature. Once you know to
look for them
you can find
them in all
sorts of places.

How many spiral shapes
can you spot in this scene?
Check your answers on
page 32.

Take inspiration from these spirals and draw some of your own spiral art.

27

SYMMETRY

Many things in nature are symmetrical. That means that two halves are exactly the same. Butterflies are symmetrical because each half has exactly the same pattern. Snowflakes are even more specially symmetrical because it doesn't matter where you divide them in two, each half will always be symmetrical.

Make these snowflakes symmetrical. Add your own designs to each 'prong' but make sure you match the design on each one.

Make the other half of these butterflies symmetrical by copying the patterns and colors you can see onto the blank wing.

BEAUTIFUL GEOMETRY

Geometry is a part of mathematics that is all about shapes. So many beautiful patterns can be made with shapes, and using some simple art skills – like coloring and drawing lines – can make them more beautiful and also help to show off the shapes inside the patterns even more clearly.

Look at these circles and all the patterns made up inside them and as a group. Color them in to show off the shapes. Think about what colors will make them look good as a group — all shades of one color? Perhaps a rainbow?

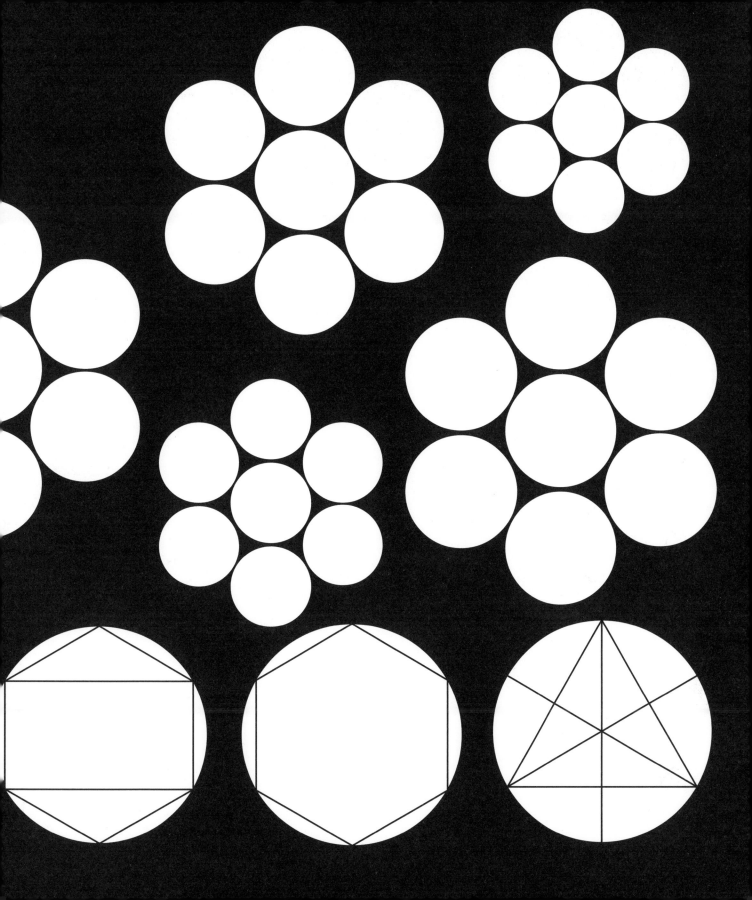

ANSWERS

page 4-5 ---->

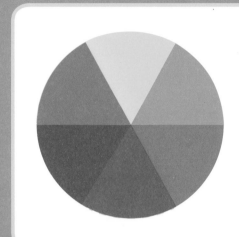

Complementary color pairs are made up of one primary color paired with the other two primary colors mixed together. Complementary color pairs are opposite each other on a color wheel.

page 26 ---->

bats

koala

star

giraffe

train

page 24-25 ---